THE PRINCESS
Diary

Título original: Princess diary, my first diary

©kaito Chen, 2017
Diseño de portada: Kaito Chen
Encuadernación: Kaito Chen
Este libro fue publicado en Amazon el 5 de Enero de 2017
ISBN — 13: 987-1542329224
ISBN — 10: 1542329221

THE PRINCESS
Diary

THE PRINCESS
Diary

THE PRINCESS
Diary

THE PRINCESS
Diary

THE PRINCESS
Diary

THE PRINCESS Diary

THE PRINCESS
Diary

THE PRINCESS Diary

THE PRINCESS
Diary

THE PRINCESS
Diary

THE PRINCESS
Diary

THE PRINCESS
Diary

THE PRINCESS
Diary

THE PRINCESS
Diary

THE PRINCESS

Diary

THE PRINCESS
Diary

THE PRINCESS
Diary

THE PRINCESS
Diary

THE PRINCESS
Diary

THE PRINCESS
Diary

THE PRINCESS
Diary